INVISIBLE ONE

INVISIBLE ONE

MARGARET FRANK

for those who have moments of feeling unseen

Standing
unseen
in front of so many variables

Power to stabilize and transform

Waking
selflessly
in the dark

So others may eat

Walking
cloaked
in anonymity

Obligations rush

Working
endlessly
on the mundane

But necessary for more than survival

Cooking
Cleaning
Civilizing

Teaching
Talking
Training

Serving
Saving
Simplifying

Building
Binding
Bypassing

externally

Digging
Sculpting
Welding

Weaving
Knitting
Embroidering

internally

Driving
in circles
time and again

Shuttling the needs of others

Feeling
powerless
the trap of decay

There are other ones
ready
      willing
            charged
to help

Waiting with purpose

Concealed
with understanding

Grieving
entrapped
by the hidden

Unburdening
others
as fast as possible

Footing
negative
Still with the power to reverse inequality

Revealing truth

Halting
alert
with steel visage

Unwavering resolve

Encouraging
tenaciously
in wanton mettle

For the collective breath

Clawing
desperately
against indifference

Holding
steady
the head

Suppressing
with strained muscle
the emotions

Tied to thankless work

Screaming
in stillness
unheard

Ready to turn it all upside down

Wrestling
recondite
with the now

Breaking
in silence
to create something new

Stretching
with agony
to make dreams come true

Collapsing
exhausted
from etching peace

On hearts of stone

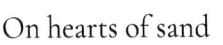
On hearts of sand

Curling
inward with grit
locating depths

Beyond vision

Rising
expectant
with diligence

Shaping the future

Raising
to one
is oneself

The foundation confirmed

Gazing
outward
with longing eyes

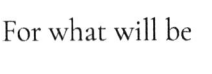
For what will be

Dissolving
relaxed
into the verity of love

Hoping
to combine
to be greater

Whole
reminded

They are part of one

Living
lightly
in humble hope

Sitting
thawed
vibrating with meaning

Unlocking answers

There is always an answer

The equation is not balanced without you.